God in
Your Morning

Ashley Ormon

Proverbs & Wisdom

God loves you no matter
what and His arms are always
opened to you.

Ashley Ormon

God in Your Morning

Copyright © 2014 by Ashley Ormon

Scripture quotations marked "KJV" are taken from the Holy Bible, King James Version, Cambridge, 1769.

Unless noted otherwise, all Scriptures are taken from the Holy Bible, New International Version, NIV. Copyright 1973, 1978, 1984, 2011 by Biblica, Inc. Used by permission of Zondervan. All rights reserved worldwide. www.zondervan.com.

The "NIV" and "New International Version" are trademarks registered in the United States Patent and Trademark Office by Biblica, Inc. Please note that Proverbs & Wisdom's publishing style capitalizes certain pronouns that refer to God, Jesus Christ, and the Holy Spirit.

Cover design: Heather Heinzer and Jennifer Maloney
Formatting by RikHall.com

For information, please visit Proverbs & Wisdom at http://www.proverbsnwisdom.comor contact@proverbsnwisdom.com.

ISBN-10:0615991033
ISBN-13:978-0-615-99103-0

Praise for *God in Your Morning*

"*God in Your Morning* is a beautiful reminder of how waking up each morning is indeed a blessing from God. Ashley Ormon opens her heart and spirit with a wonderful combination of thought-provoking devotionals, combined with scripture and prayer. It will be a blessing to all who make it a part of their daily walk with the Lord."

—Matt Patterson, Inspirational Speaker and author of *My Emily*

"*God in Your Morning* is a well-written, wisdom-packed and uplifting devotional. It will help you be filled with peace, joy and hope. As you read, expect your days to unfold beautifully and see your life change for the best as you digest its truths. I give this 10 thumbs up! I can't wait to read Ashley's next devotional!"

—Serge Roux-Levrat, Principal Ambassador of SRL Ministries, Author of *Spiritually Stronger in 40 days*!

"*God in Your Morning* is beyond beautiful. It's absolutely a divine read. It's touching, full of wisdom and inspiration. A book I'd definitely recommend to all."

—Joie Schmidt, Poet and author of *Dreams of the Heart Vol. I & II* and *Love in a Heart Locket*

"*God in Your Morning* is wonderful to start your day with by helping you draw closer to the Lord. Each message is informative and uplifting. I highly recommend this well-written, inspiring devotional. No matter where you are in your walk with Christ, you will be blessed by this book."

—Amanda Beth, author of *You Can Have a Happy Family* and *The LOVE Walk*

Dedication

To anyone:

For all with the desire to bring God into their morning

Acknowledgments

It is always a privilege and a special blessing to have people to whom I can say, "Thank you."

Therefore, for these individuals I am forever grateful:

First and foremost, my heavenly Father God who gifted me to write. I am a writer, but God is the author. To Jesus Christ, my Lord and Savior, for His unfailing love. Praise you.

To my mother and father, Jeffrey and Rocal, who have supported me in countless ways. Dad, thank you for your listening ears and all the suggestions you have provided. Mom, I recall those days you prayed with me every morning and said after waking up, before I did anything else, talk to God. To my intermediate and extended family, thank you.

To Proverbs & Wisdom's staff for their willingness to serve not me, but God and others. Your prayers and lessons of faith has blessed me and allowed us all to touch many lives.

To my wonderful editors, Katheryn Lane and Susan Dusterhoft, who guided me word-by-word through the editorial process. Without you two, this book would not be presented as well. Susan, thank you for sharing your expertise with me in becoming a better writer.

To the pastors at Word of Life Ministries for their guidance and mentorship. To Pastor Steve and Pastor Fred, thank you for sharing your godly wisdom.

To my friends, Amanda and Dominique, for their constant support. Amanda, if it were not for you suggesting I publish *God in Your Morning*, it may have remained a manuscript. To Dominique, thank you for all the prayers and support you have given.

To my high school friend, Lisa Quigley, who always encouraged me and referred to me as "Miss Writer." You always did tell me and others that one day, I would write a book. Thank you.

To all unnamed, please know that your contributions are not valued any less. As Paul says, "I thank my God always on your behalf, for the grace of God which is given you by Jesus Christ (1 Corinthians 1:4 KJV)." Your love, support and prayers are appreciated.

Contents

Let the morning bring me word of your unfailing love,
for I have put my trust in you.
Show me the way I should go,
for to you I entrust my life.

~ Psalms 143:8

Introduction

Waking up every morning is a blessing from God. Each day enables us to enjoy more opportunities, gifts, and wonders life has to offer; but our mornings begin that journey, making it the most — if not *the* most — important part of our day.

Starting your day properly is easy: begin it with God. By doing so, a foundation of hope, joy, and peace is created. This does not ensure that your day will be perfect, but it does make it easier. I understand our mornings can be busy; however, if we cannot make time for God now, then when? *God in Your Morning* is designed to be read two pages per day. God designated time to wake us up; the *least* we can do is include Him in our mornings.

Every page will begin with a scripture and a short article after it reflecting on the verse(s) chosen for that day. And if you stop reading, you can return where you left off. The days aren't specific to the date of the year; instead they are labeled as "Day 1,""Day 2," and so forth.

Remember too, after each passage it is good to end with prayer. Each page will end with a prayer, but I encourage you to add one of your own. God loves listening to what *you* have to say!

I hope you are blessed by the following pages. May they help you begin your day the right way — with God.

Ashley Ormon

Day One

Know that the LORD has set apart the godly for himself; the LORD will hear when I call to him.
~Psalms 4:3

I value everything I write, with my poems and novel drafts holding the most importance. Instead of keeping them with the rest of my papers filed away or placed elsewhere, I set them apart. They are all placed in a special binder with sheet protectors over them. It is because of their significant value to me that I place them above all the rest.

In God's eyes you aren't any different. He set you apart, within His presence to be sheltered and protected, because you are precious to Him. As the apple of His eyes, He listens to your every word. Whether fear, pain or joy—anything else it may be—He is always listening.

How do I know? In Isaiah 65:24 God says, "Before they call I will answer; while they are still speaking I will hear." When you speak to the Creator, be assured that He is listening, happy that you are talking to Him.

This morning, spend at least five minutes with God. He set everything aside to be with you. How wonderful would it be for you to do the same! Speak to Him. When you're praying, you don't have to use elaborate words or speak in a specific way. Be respectful, but be yourself. The easiest way to pray to God is by having a conversation. Talk to Him as you would anyone else. Remember, He's listening to your prayer.

Today's Prayer:
Good Morning God,

Thank you for waking me up this morning. I invite you into my day. I understand that not everyone was granted the gift of today and I appreciate this blessing. Please allow me to honor you in all I do today, and provide me with the strength I need to make it through this day. As your child who has been set apart, teach me how to maintain that separation. Allow me not to place myself in circumstances that will conjoin me with the very things from which you have placed me away. Lord, I just want to thank you for all you do for me each and every morning. I love you. In Jesus' name, amen.

Day Two

Come and listen, all you who fear God; let me tell you what he has done for me.

~Psalms 66:16

Throughout the Bible from the Old to the New Testament you'll read that God despises the proud, but loves and blesses the humble. Everything we own, receive, and obtain comes from God. Looking at life in this perspective makes it easy to understand why we aren't to be proud. We are who we are and have what we have only by the grace of God.

However, the Bible does say we are permitted to boast about God (Jeremiah 9:24). When we joyfully assert what God has done for us, people are led closer to Him. I once experienced this when a friend of mine asked why I was so happy. I was coming out of a "dry place," and my life was finally turning around. I could have recounted many wonderful things, yet I didn't. Instead I told him, "God is so good. He's given me so much joy. I was going through a hard time, but look what He did with the situation." After hearing so much about the goodness of God he asked me to tell him more about God. My friend saw what I had, and wanted to know what God could do for him.

There's a story about two men — one wealthy and the other poor. The wealthy man was speaking of everything he had — a yacht, mansions, and luxurious cars. The poor man, not intimidated by the wealthy man's boasting replied, "Well, my Father owns everything. He's rich. Where He lives the streets are paved with gold. He has more than enough. People praise Him!" Surprised, the wealthy man inquired of the poor man's father. The poor man responded, "God." Similar to the poor man, boast about God's glory to others this morning! Speak of His goodness.

Today's Prayer:
Good Morning God,

Thank you for waking me up today and for your loving-kindness towards me. I thank you that even when I am not good to you, you still show mercy and favor towards me. Help me not to be ashamed of all the wonderful blessings you have provided and to speak of your glory. Allow others to be touched by all the work you are doing through me. In Jesus' name, amen.

Day Three

Trust in the Lord with all your heart and lean not on your own understanding; in all your ways acknowledge him, and he will make your paths straight.
                    ~Proverbs 3:5-6

The above scripture has to be one of the most commonly recited. While this may be good, it does have its disadvantages. Sometimes when we hear things repeatedly, it can lose its significance to us.Let's look at this verse more closely:

•*Trust in the Lord with all your heart*: We should place all of our trust in God and trust Him with all things. We shouldn't just trust Him in bad times (e.g., times of financially instability or uncertainty about a decision.) Instead we should trust Him at all times.

•*Lean not on your own understanding*: God's knowledge and understanding surpasses ours more than we could ever imagine. He's omniscient. In every circumstance we need to depend on God's all-knowing wisdom. He holds the blue-print and when we listen and obey His words, we are shown prosperity.

•*In all your ways acknowledge him*: Do we pay attention to God sometimes or all the time? When we're out enjoying our day do we think of Him? Acknowledge all that He has done and is doing in our lives. Think of God when you feel the cool breeze, or when seeing a child smile. Recognize His presence.

•*And he will make your paths straight*: God reveals the benefits of trusting, acknowledging, and depending on Him.

Today's Prayer:
Good Morning God,

Thank you for waking me up this morning. Thank you for allowing me to be able to trust in you fully. Thank you for being faithful to me. Today, now and forevermore help me to acknowledge you in all that I do. Help me to seek your understanding and to use it wisely. In Jesus' name, amen.

Day Four

And what does the LORD require of you? To act justly and to love
mercy and to walk humbly with your God.
~Micah 6:8

It amazes me how well trained we are in following the world's rules. We stop at red lights, slow down at yellow lights and when the light turns green, we don't hesitate for the slightest second to "go."

Yet, when God gives us rules, we don't always obey His instructions. Is God's law not greater than the ones the world tells us to follow? Jobs have requirements and we follow them. We require others to be honest and forthright with us. While we expect others to meet those standards, God also expects the same of us.

Right now, consider how many standards and requirements you have to abide by whether it is of your spouse, children, friends, employer, or yourself. Now, consider the requirements God has for you. It's only four: to act justly at all times, to love and be merciful (forgiving), and lastly, to be humble before Him.

Meet these expectations during the course of your day. If you forget or have a hard time doing so, don't worry. Continue trying. As cliché as it may sound, practice does make perfect. And like anything else you do continuously, it'll become a habit.

Today's Prayer:
Good Morning God,

Thank you for waking me up today. I invite you into my morning and into my day. Please be a part of it. Lord, I understand that you have specific expectations and requirements of me. Enable me to abide by them. Teach me how to walk in love. In all that I do may I display mercy and maintain a humble attitude. Remind me during times of forgetfulness. Lord, I want to honor and obey you. Thank you for your help today. In Jesus' name, amen.

Day Five

Depart, depart, go out from there! Touch no unclean thing! Come out from it and be pure, you who carry the vessels of the Lord.
~Isaiah 52:11

I'll never forget my last week of high school. At the academy I attended it was mandatory for all the girls to wear white for each special ceremony we were having before and the day of graduation.

Seeing that our dresses, shoes, and caps and gowns were all white, all the girls were concerned about getting dirty. The hall we had our luncheon at had beautiful benches outside with waterfalls behind them. It was the perfect place to take photos.

No one wanted to sit down out of the fear of getting dirty. Instead, we enjoyed the fresh air standing up and quickly returned inside where it was much cleaner.

That experience reminds me of this scripture. "Depart" refers to us leaving the unclean (outside) to remain clean ("pure"). We refrained from sitting on the beautiful benches ("touch no unclean thing") in order to keep our dresses white. As extreme as this reference may seem, this is God's desire for us. He wants us to be pure, touching and surrounding ourselves only with goodness.

This morning, keep Isaiah 52:11 in mind. Seek what is pure and surround yourself in it. You belong to a clean and righteous God, and as His child, He wants you to be the same.

Today's Prayer:
Good Morning God,

Thank you for waking me up. Today, I invite you to come into my morning. I welcome your presence, love and Spirit to be here with me. Guide my steps away from all impurities and make me holy to you. Help me to recognize all things which are not from you nor pleasant to do. Please give me the discernment to know what is righteous and pure, and what is not. Thank you. In Jesus' name, amen.

Day Six

Yet, O LORD, you are our Father. We are the clay, you are the potter; we are all the work of your hand.
~Isaiah 64:8

Did you know God made you the way you are on purpose? He gave you the gifts and talents you have for a reason. As the scripture says above, God is the potter, making and molding us into who He wants us to be.

I don't have too much experience in pottery, but I have seen it done. It truly is a great art form. It takes patience and skill. The details the artists put into their clay amazes me. They literally take a big ball of unformed clay, and turn it into a beautiful object. Unlike a painter who uses a brush or other artists who use tools, a potter uses nothing but his bare hands. How awesome is it then that we were all crafted by God's hands? It was with His palms, His fingers, His creativity, that we were all molded into who we are. Ephesians 2:10 says, "For we are God's workmanship, created in Christ Jesus to do good works, which God prepared in advance for us to do."

Today, rejoice knowing that you are God's masterpiece and were created by His planned vision. You may have some imperfections that you are trying to improve, but God is still molding you. Just be assured that when He is finished, you'll be beautifully and wonderfully crafted by His hands.

Today's Prayer:
Good Morning God,

I appreciate you waking me up. It's a blessing knowing you have crafted me by hand and I am your workmanship. Allow me to appreciate everything you created me to be, and to never take the gifts and talents you've given me for granted. Today, show me how to glorify you. In Jesus' name, amen.

Day Seven

You will seek me and find me when you seek me with all you heart.
~ Jeremiah 29:13

God's word is always true. It never contradicts itself. In Matthew, Jesus says "seek and you shall find (Matthew 7:7)" and here, even before Jesus walked the earth, we see that God says if we seek Him, we will find Him.

During the previous devotions you've read that the Bible says "in *all* your ways acknowledge him" and to "trust in the Lord with *all* your heart." God wants you to give your all—not just go halfway. No one wants a partially done job or a person who is only half committed to them. God doesn't expect anything less from us.

Right now, seek God with your entire heart. Let Him know you are committed. You wouldn't want to be in a relationship with someone who was only halfway committed to you, so don't treat God with any less respect. Give Him everything.

Put your life in His hands. I am certain that if you do, you will be in the best hands possible!

Today's Prayer:
Good Morning God,

Thank you for loving me and blessing me with a brand new day! Lord, today I want to commit my life to you. I want your perfect will to be done in my life. I give you my heart and everything within me. Lord, I do not want to be half-committed to you. I want to be completely yours. God, I know that because I am wholeheartedly seeking you, your presence will be upon me. Thank you. In Jesus' name, amen.

Day Eight

His dominion is an everlasting dominion that will not pass away, and his kingdom is one that will never be destroyed.
~ Daniel 7:14

This scripture is exciting to read, and knowing that we are a part of God's everlasting kingdom is even more exciting. Buildings and oceans that were once beautiful have been destroyed and changed, but the kingdom we are part of will always be wonderful.

No matter how happy or unhappy you woke up today, praise God with the understanding that He chose you to be part of a permanent, glorious kingdom. Let this be the reason for your joy regardless of how wonderful or awful your day is. Let the joy flow through you.

Kings have risen and kings have fallen. Kingdoms and royal families that were destined to last forever failed. Princes and rulers lost control over their people. Yet, God is not like us. He is all-powerful ruling forever and ever.

Today's Prayer:
Good Morning God,

Thank you for the gift of today! You are so wonderful and mighty! Thank you for choosing me to be a part of the everlasting kingdom you have established and reign over. May I always dwell in your presence and remain a citizen of heaven. I am glad that after kingdoms fall, and the earth perishes, I will be able to call your Kingdom my home. Please remind me of this throughout the day and let the joy of your love reside in me. Thank you. In Jesus' name, amen.

Day Nine

The LORD your God is with you, he is mighty to save. He will take great delight in you, he will quiet you with his love, he will rejoice over you with singing.

                    ~Zephaniah 3:17

Comfort is found in this verse. I love the part which reads "…he will quiet you with his love." The earliest parts of our day can become busy; rushing against time, making sure we don't leave the house without any necessities, trying to eat breakfast and for some, working out in the morning. Reading this verse shows us that amidst all the "hustle and bustle," God will give us peace through His love.

In the scripture, all it speaks about is God *and* you. Specifically, what God will do for you. "God is with *you*…He will…delight in *you*…he will quiet *you*…he will rejoice over *you*" (italics mine). It displays what God wants to do for us. He wants to rejoice over us and pour out His love.

If you woke up today with feelings of worry or anxiety, know that God is "mighty to save"; if you woke up feeling unhappy, understand that God "will take great delight in you" and "will rejoice over you with singing"; if you're stressed this morning, find peace knowing God will "quiet you with his love."

Today's Prayer:
Good Morning God,

Thank you for blessing me with today. Thank you for the everlasting peace and great joy you have provided me. Thank you for being with me and spreading your love within and near me. I appreciate all you have done and all that you will do. In Jesus' name, amen.

Day Ten

In the morning, O Lord, you hear my voice; in the morning I lay my requests before you and wait in expectation.
~Psalms 5:3

How many times do we ask God for things; constantly pray over and over, and yet doubt He will do it? King David said in Psalms 5:3 that he gave His requests to God and waited in expectation. David believed whatever he wanted to get was possible. It was just going to take time. He didn't have any second thoughts his requests were impossible. He knew if he was patience, eventually they would come.

More than anything, doubt and our discouraged attitudes prevent us from obtaining our blessings. We harbor feelings of doubt before our blessings can even reach us.

Sometimes people tend to get discouraged out of impatience because they haven't received their desires quickly enough. But this, my friends, is an attitude we have to overcome.

Knowing that all things require time, I encourage you to have faith. Trust in God, and wait in expectation today that He will answer your requests when the time is right. Say, "Lord, I trust your understanding and the timing you have planned for every person and everyone. Today, I will wait on you."

Today's Prayer:
Good Morning God,

Thank you for today. Before I begin anything, I invite you to become a part of my day. Lord, please take away any fear and doubt I may carry. Please do not let anything—not even myself—hinder the blessings you have for me. In Jesus' name, amen.

Day Eleven

But the fruit of the Spirit is love, joy, peace, patience, kindness, goodness, faithfulness, gentleness and self-control. Against such things there is no law.

~ *Galatians 5:22-23*

If you've been around long enough, you've probably heard the saying "you are what you eat." This is true, but I will revise this, "You are also what you plant." If you plant an apple seed, what will grow? Of course, you will get an apple tree.

Just as an apple seed is planted and then produces fruit, so do you. Except your "fruits" are not edible like an apple or orange. They are the characteristics you possess.

If you are unsure which fruit you struggle producing, answer the questions below. Remember, the more you practice bearing them, the more natural it'll become.

1. Do you hold grudges and have a hard time forgiving? Work on love.
2. Are you depressed, ungrateful, or unsatisfied with life? Work on joy.
3. Do you argue a lot, look for trouble, or try to cause problems? Work on peace.
4. Do you have a problem with waiting or always trying to rush? Work on patience.
5. Are you selfish or rude? Work on kindness.
6. Do you do wrong purposely or try to cause harm?

Work on goodness.

7. Do you stay true to your word? Are you dependable? Work on faithfulness.
8. Are you a mean person? Work on gentleness.
9. Are you easily angered? Work on self-control.

Today's Prayer:
Good Morning God,

Thank you for today. Help me to bear the fruits of the Spirit. May I always be a good tree bearing righteous fruit. Help me to possess Godly characteristics. May the fruit of the Spirit become embedded into my character and become part of my daily lifestyle. In Jesus' name, amen.

Day Twelve

Therefore I tell you, do not worry about your life.
~ Matthew 6:25a

What are you worrying about? Do you not know you serve and belong to the Almighty? God loves you and He will provide you with all of your needs. In Matthew 6:25-31, Jesus says if God will take care of the birds and nature then He will take care of you even more.

In Matthew 6:8, Christ tells us God knows your needs before you ask Him! Just because you may not see a provision during difficult times, doesn't mean God is unaware. In times when you feel inclined to worry, talk to God. Ask Him for whatever it is you need and then, believe He will supply it.

We tend to worry when our trust in God deceases. Yet, standing in full confidence of His capabilities makes the unnecessary worrying and anxiety fade away. Our troubles and needs may be in abundance, but God owns all and creates all.

How upset it must make God that after all He has done for you, you are still worrying about how you will manage. After all the blessings, the gifts, and days of life He has given you there shouldn't be a question in your mind if God will come through or not.

Trust me my friend, God will surely not leave you alone when you are in need.

Today's Prayer:
Good Morning God,

Thank you for this morning and providing for me. Thank you for being present in my life daily, and for allowing me to come to you when I am in need. Help me to not only seek you when I am in despair, but in all circumstances. Please take all feelings of worry, anxiety, and fear out of my life. Help me to be courageous; walking in full confidence of everything you are capable. Enable me to trust in you and understand that my needs will be met. I just have to be patient enough to let you provide for me. In Jesus' name, amen.

Day Thirteen

Be still and know that I am God.
~ Psalms 46:10

Sometimes we just need to rest in the presence of God, acknowledging He is Lord of our lives and every living thing. The best part of my day is sitting still, being quiet, and resting in God's presence. There is a great comfort in knowing God is doing exactly what He wants to do — be our Father. He wants to hold you, love you, and bless you abundantly.

I often think of situations I have gone through in the past and I now understand if I had only let God be God, the circumstance would have been much easier. Every day, throughout your day, just take out time to be with God. Permit Him to work in you and through you. Surrender yourself.

You'll be amazed at the overflowing peace that overtakes you; the overflow of joy that will fill you. The overflow of love that God will just pour and pour and pour deep within your bones — circulating to every part of your body.

This morning, let God's Spirit be upon you. Turn off the television, silence your phone, and even if it is only for five minutes — be still. Recognize that He is God.

Today's Prayer:
Good Morning God,

Thank you for waking me up this morning. I sit still before you humbled, recognizing that you are Lord. Make your way into my life. Pour your Spirit upon me and allow me to receive everything you are offering to me. In Jesus' name, amen.

Day Fourteen

By faith we understand that the universe was formed at God's command,
so that what is seen was not made out of what was visible.
~ Hebrews 11:3

The foundations of the earth were established upon faith. It is because of faith and through faith that we can believe what Christ has done for us and be saved. The Bible says without faith, it is impossible to please God (Hebrews 11:6).

By believing in what we cannot see, we can have hope good things will come into existence. We can be assured that with God, anything is possible. Having faith permits us to see ourselves victorious in all our circumstances and allows us to envision something much better than what is in our present. Through faith, we can walk in all of God's promises and His perfect will for our lives. We may not see it just yet, but by believing it, we are placing it into our future.

In the book of Matthew, chapter fourteen, the story of Peter is told. Peter's faith was so strong he was able to walk on water. The minute he lost faith, he doubted and began to drown. It was proven to Peter it *was* possible to walk on water and what he wanted to do *could* be achieved, but he lost faith. My friends don't be like Peter and lose faith especially after God has proven to you what you are capable of.

Today's Prayer:
Good Morning God,

Thank you for being in my life and giving me another day. For now and forever, help me to believe. Increase my faith in the things you are capable of doing and will do in my life. Prevent me from being like Peter, who had strong faith within you and then doubted. Let me not live life in disbelief, but in assurance that with you, all things are possible. In Jesus' name, amen.

Day Fifteen

There is surely a future hope for you, and your hope will not be cut off.
~ Proverbs 23:18

We can lose hope in times of struggles and hardships, but we must remember we are capable of overcoming all things. Nothing is impossible. And if we believe we can do it, we can. We can't let our problems defeat us. Instead, we must defeat our problems. Normally our situations appear bigger than they really are. It isn't until we change our view of them that they become easier and more manageable to work through.

Everyone goes through issues in life so don't feel discouraged. Usually, if it weren't for our struggles, we wouldn't be the strong individuals we are presently. Whenever you feel like a task is impossible to do, remember past issues you have gone through. Remember how you once struggled, found the solution and overcame it. The milestone you are facing now is the same. It is only a stepping-stone which will take you to higher places in life.

Be encouraged! God has something great planned for you. Often, people give up without knowing success was just around the corner; if they had only persevered a little bit longer, if they had only tried one more time, they could have succeeded. You may not see success right now, but know it exists. Know God has blessed you with a prosperous future (Jeremiah 29:11).

Today's Prayer:
Good Morning God,

Thank you for giving me everlasting hope. Encourage me to conquer the difficulties I face. Help me to not feel crestfallen in bad times, but rejoice knowing these challenges will help me to improve in my walk with you. Thank you for all you have done, are doing, and will do in the future. In Jesus' name, amen.

Day Sixteen

Humble yourselves before the Lord, and he will lift you up.
~ James 4:10

I'm sure you've heard or recited the saying "actions speak louder than words." If you are doing something positive, if you are successful, whatever it may be — people are going to notice. Why? Because actions speak. When you are doing well, there is never a reason to boast or be proud, people will notice. Besides, if you are going to be honored, let it be by someone else, not yourself. Praise from others is valued more.

The Bible shows us the importance of maintaining a humble attitude. Satan, who was once an angel in Heaven, became too proud and therefore, was cast out. God loves a humble attitude. In fact, He honors it and despises the proud (Proverbs 29:23).

The character you have today, is it humble or proud? You will not be uplifted by God unless you live a lifestyle of humility. If this becomes a struggle for you, never forget you can always ask God to help you.

Today's Prayer:
Good Morning God,

Lord, thank you for waking me up this morning. Please help me to be humble and resist any thoughts filled with pride. Lord, let me not only be humble before you, but humble when I am with others. Please do not allow my ego and the things I have accomplished prohibit me from being pleasing in your eyes. I place my life into your hands. In Jesus' name, amen.

Day Seventeen

Then you will experience God's peace, which exceeds anything we can understand. His peace will guard your hearts and minds as you live in Christ Jesus.

~ Philippians 4:7

There is a peace — an everlasting peace — that passes all understanding, overcomes all stress, and will remain within us forever. Normally we find that peace is temporary. We find it by taking a brisk walk outside, or finding a place to be alone, and after these moments are done we find ourselves returning back to an unsound mind.

Jesus said, "Peace be with you." When Peter and John, disciples of Jesus, wrote their scriptures, they ended each with "Peace to all of you" and "Peace to you." Notice that they didn't say "peace when you go out or anywhere else." They said, "Peace be with *you*." The reason you don't have an everlasting peace is because you haven't searched where it exists — in you.

The Bible says God has given you peace, power, and a sound mind. If He has given it to you, why not receive it? Inner peace is the most precious peace of all. All it requires is for you to receive it and bring it out from within.

Today's Prayer:
Good Morning God,

Thank you for your peace which passes all understanding. As I start my day today, please help me bring your peace wherever I may travel. Keep all stress and all frustration away from me. Let me be able to bring peace to others; helping them and encouraging them. I ask all of this in Jesus' name, amen.

Day Eighteen

In everything set them an example by doing what is good. In your teaching show integrity, seriousness and soundness of speech that cannot be condemned, so that those who oppose you may be ashamed because they having nothing bad to say about us.
~Titus 2:6-8

When I took dance classes, one of the older girls would always say, "People are going to talk. Might as well give them something good to talk about." I don't know if that's an original quote or not, but that isn't the point. It has great truths within it.

There will always be individuals who seek our ruin, who are looking to "bad mouth" us and want to put us down. I like the verse above because it says if we walk, act and speak in an upright manner, people will not have anything bad to say about us.

It explains that our very existence should be an example to others: to live with integrity. We should not pick and choose the moments to lead by example, but "in everything" display "what is good."

This morning, be God's representative. Have God in your morning by displaying His glory in you. When others see you today, may your very life be an example of what God, our Father, is like.

Today's Prayer:
Good Morning God,

Thank you for another day. Thank you for being such a great example of how I ought to act every day of my life. When I do wrong, please correct me so I won't lead others astray. Let my life be a living example on how all people should act towards you, themselves and others. In Jesus' name, amen.

Day Nineteen

Be wise in the way you act toward outsiders; make the most of every opportunity.
~ *Colossians 4:5*

It's ironic that some of the most judgmental people I've met are those who define themselves as righteous, Christians, good people, kindhearted and loving.

And it breaks my heart every single day to see Christians turning away the very people Jesus Christ came to save.

John 3:16 says, "For God so loved the world." It doesn't read: for God so loved the church, the righteous ones, the holy ones and so forth. God loved the world with such a great passion that He sent His Son, Jesus, to deliver the lost and brokenhearted.

The way we conduct ourselves should lead others to God. Christ called us to be His ambassadors. Unbelievers are watching and if we aren't being Christ-like they could form a negative impression of who Christ truly is. How terrible would it be if people viewed God and Christ as judgmental and unkind because we as their representatives are displaying ungodly characteristics?

This morning, examine yourself. Change your attitude and your ways if necessary. Think of the characteristics God embodies: love, joy, forgiveness, kindness—and then, try to display these characteristics to others.

Today's Prayer:
Good Morning God,

Thank you waking me up today. Lord, help me not to push away people. Help me to be a true representation of who you and your son are. May the things I say and do bring others closer to your heart. Please allow me to use every opportunity to display your glory. In Jesus' name, amen.

Day Twenty

Create in me a pure heart, O God, and renew a steadfast spirit within me.

~ *Psalm 51:10*

Ever since I was a little girl, I've had a fish tank. The funny thing is, despite my current fish tank being 55 gallons of water, it still gets dirty. About every five to six months I have to drain the water, clean the rocks and scrub the inside of the tank. In addition, about every three to four months, the filters need to be changed.

It always starts out clean and yet time after time, it still manages to have some impurities within it. Our heart is the same way. We have to ask God often to clean our heart and mind. Even if God cleaned our heart yesterday, some impurities may have started to form in us since then.

The heart is the most important part of the body. Proverbs 4:23 reads, "Above all else, guard your heart, for it is the wellspring of life." Meaning, everything we do is a product of what is in our heart. Jesus said in Matthew 5:11, it is the things within our heart that causes us to do unrighteousness. In Matthew 12:34, we learn, "Out of the abundance of the heart, the mouth speaks."

Today, ask God to "cleanse" your heart. Permit Him to remove all impurities, wash you from the inside out and make you pure. And pray for a steadfast spirit—one that will be loyal and faithful to God.

Today's Prayer:
Good Morning God,

Thank you for waking me up today. Lord, please clean my heart and cleanse me from all unrighteousness. Bless me to walk in your ways, to follow your instructions and to seek your righteousness. In Jesus' name, amen.

Day Twenty-One

For it is better, if it is God's will, to suffer for doing good than for doing evil.

~ *1 Peter 3:17*

Little children are famous for saying "it's not fair." And as they mature into adults, they ask the question many people before them have sought an answer to: why do bad things happen to good people?

It can become discouraging too if you take special care into doing what's right and still suffer. Some may even ask, "What's the point? Why walk in righteousness and suffer when you can do what you want and still have hardships?"

Peter responds, it is better to be in righteousness and suffer, than to go against God by doing evil and *still* suffer. The Beatitudes in Matthew 5 send out comfort to good-doers. Jesus says, "Blessed are those who are persecuted because of righteousness, for theirs is the kingdom of heaven." The most exciting part is that Jesus talks in the present tense. He doesn't say "for theirs *will be* the kingdom of heaven" (italics mine). He says, "For theirs *is* the kingdom of heaven" (italics mine). Right now, on earth, the kingdom of Heaven is yours.

When you suffer for doing good, or when your kindness is taken for granted, don't harden your heart and vow never to be kind again. Instead, recall the words of Jesus and view it as a blessing. Smile knowing your reward doesn't come from the good you do for others. It comes from God in Heaven.

Today's Prayer:
Good Morning God,

I love you! Thank you for creating a new day for me to live in. Today put a helping and kind-hearted spirit within me. Give me the desire to do good under all circumstances. If I suffer for being righteous, please remind me to continue doing your work and not to do evil. Comfort me and bless me to have a great day. In Jesus' name, amen.

Day Twenty-Two

Now faith is confidence in what we hope for and assurance about what we do not see.
~ Hebrews 11: 1

Looking at the present can be depressing sometimes. The glass seems to be half full, or worse — completely empty. I'm referring to those days you can't seem to find a way out, all your hope seems to have diminished, you have things you want to accomplish, but you're wondering if it's even possible.

I know and I understand. I've had those days. I've been a victim. And when discouraging thoughts such as these come to mind, I force myself to remember Hebrews chapter 11 which states "by faith" great men and women did miraculous works, not because they saw them happening, but because they *believed* and *hoped* that they could. I remember 2 Corinthians 4:8 which says we should fix our eyes on the unseen because what we see is temporary. I think of Romans 4:17 which says God calls into being things that aren't as if they were. I encourage myself understanding although I cannot see a way, if I have hope and believe, it can come to pass.

Trust me, I've had times when I've hit rock bottom. I've had those mornings when I've woken up feeling completely and entirely empty. However, God has encouraged me and He will encourage you. When things in your life seem pointless, hopeless or impossible, be encouraged and empowered that with God, you can achieve.

By committing what you do to God, your plans will succeed (Proverbs 16:3). Your success has been predestined by God, and if you have enough hope, in due time you'll be able to walk in it abundantly.

Today's Prayer:
Good Morning God,

Please help encourage me to do greater things in life. Father, impart the wisdom within me that my current struggles are just preparing me for a greater glory. Help me to have hope, to persevere and be determined in all things. Uplift my spirit. Place a soundtrack of positive words within me. Thank you for all you have and will do.In Jesus' name, amen.

Day Twenty-Three

Whatever you do, work at it with all your heart, as working for the Lord, not for human masters, since you know that you will receive an inheritance from the Lord as a reward. It is the Lord Christ you are serving.

~ *Colossians 3:23-24*

Each scripture in the Bible is a key to success, but this scripture is one of my "personal life verses" for becoming successful. It wasn't until I started living according to this scripture that I prospered in the workplace. Before, I would just go to work, do what I had to do the best that I could and that was it. If I wasn't having the greatest day, I would slack a little; if my boss wasn't the nicest to me, it reflected in my work.

Then my focused changed. I started working not for my supervisors and managers, but for God. I went to work full of enthusiasm, asking my co-workers if they needed help if I wasn't too busy and I gave my boss my all. I went out of my way to do things I wasn't necessarily required to do. If I felt like "taking it easy" one day, I didn't. I continued to work for God and in turn, God worked for me by setting up blessings at my job. Within a few weeks, I qualified to take on greater tasks. My boss asked me if I could do larger projects and I noticed the more I worked for God, the more God blessed me with promotions at my job.

Today, whatever your job may be—work, student, stay-at-home mom or teacher—work for God. Yes, your boss may irritate you or be rude, or you may not like the administration at your school, but God doesn't ask you to work for them. He asks that you serve Him. And besides, God says you will receive an inheritance, one that is much greater than your paycheck!

Today's Prayer:
Good Morning God,

Thank you for all you have done. Lord, bless me to work hard and have a willing attitude. Remind me that in all I do, I am constantly working for you and your kingdom. Help to keep me from slacking. Teach me to be the servant you want me to become. In Jesus' name, amen.

Day Twenty-Four

He who guards his lips, guards his life.
~ Proverbs 13:3

If you want your life to change, you have to change the way you speak. Talking negatively is the same as doing something badly and expecting great results; chances are, it isn't going to happen. Words are meaningful and carry life within them. The smallest sentence can have the most powerful meaning. Take these short quotations for example:

- *An eye for eye only ends up making the whole world blind.*
  —*Mohandas K. Gandhi*
- *In three words I can sum up what I've learned about life: It goes on.*
  —*Robert Frost*
- *Don't compromise yourself. You are all you've got.*
  —*Janis Joplin*
- *I can do all things through Christ who strengthens me.*
  —*Philippians 4:13*

All of these sentences are short, yet each contains great truth, power and wisdom. Likewise, your words are valuable; including the ones you don't think are significant. When you talk, speak words of wisdom, words of intelligence and most of all words that uplift you and those around you. Wisdom demands attention. If your words are few yet wise, people are bound to listen.

The Bible tells us God's plans are a response from what we say (Proverbs 16:1). What words are you sending up to Heaven this morning? Did you wake up saying, "Ugh, today's going to be bad" or something of that sort? If so, take it back. Remember, guard your life by being cautious of the words you speak over it.

Today's Prayer:
Good Morning God,

Thank you for waking me up this morning. Enable me to speak words of life — words of health, favor, blessings and love. Please keep negativity out of my mouth and help me to refrain from speaking gossip and discouraging words. Lord, may the words you reply to be ones that will release everything you have for me. Thank you. In Jesus' name, amen.

Day Twenty-Five

Keep this Book of the Law always on your lips; meditate on it day and night, so that you may be careful to do everything written in it. Then you will be prosperous and successful.
~Joshua 1:8

We all want prosperity, we all desire success, and here, God tells us so perfectly how to obtain it. In studying and reading the Bible for some time now, I've realized the Bible is truly a gift for all humankind. Somehow, someway, every scripture relates to you.

We can't add to God's word, we can't add to His glory, and everything we could possibly offer God—including our life—belongs to Him. To me, the Bible is literally a roadmap, a manual, an instruction booklet on how we can make ourselves prosperous and receive the most from life. I'm sure God didn't have the Bible written for His benefit, He has infinite wisdom.

God had the Bible written for us, so that we may learn and understand life and creation as He does.

Joshua 1:8 tells us to mediate on God's word: read, listen, and study it. Why? So we can "be careful to do everything written in it." Remember, the Bible was written for you, so if God says do what's instructed, you have to believe it's going to benefit you.

This morning, spend at least ten minutes with God. Five minutes reading His word and five minutes talking to Him. I would advise fifteen to be honest, by adding five minutes to listen to God's response when you're done talking. If you aren't sure where to start, begin by reading the book of Proverbs, 1 Corinthians, John, or Ephesians. They are filled with insight.

Today's Prayer:
Good Morning God,

Thank you for today. I invite you into my morning, not to be a passive bystander, but to be an active participant in all that I do. Teach me, and impart wisdom and knowledge in me. Help me to have the mind of Christ, so that I may remember, understand and obey your word. Thank you for allowing me to have a roadmap to your kingdom. I appreciate all that you do and will do for me, now and forevermore. In Jesus' name, amen.

Day Twenty-Six

Moreover, when God gives any man wealth and possessions, and enables him to enjoy them, to accept his lot and be happy in his work—this is a gift of God.
~Ecclesiastes 5:19

Little children are very precious. And if you've had any experience of being with a young child, especially between the ages of 3 to 6 years old, you know that they *love* to show you their work. My niece often says, "Aunt Ashley, look what I did!" and if I'm not looking she'll say, "You're not looking. LOOK!" Children take joy in their work and sometimes as adults we forget that's something we should continue doing.

We aren't being vain in doing so, nor is it wrong. The Bible says it is a gift from God to be able to enjoy the fruit of your labor. I am sure within your schedule there are tasks you have accomplished. You may not have saved a life (although it is possible), but perhaps you completed smaller things. Be happy with them! I always find it too, that when I step back to enjoy something I've completed, it gives me motivation to move onto the next task. It encourages me and it helps to uplift my spirit.

Today, this morning, think of all the things you have accomplished. Enjoy them. Love what you do and rejoice knowing you have achieved. Smile. Even if you don't get much completed this week, you can always have the joy of knowing there are many things you have done and are still capable of doing.

Today's Prayer:
Good Morning God,

Thank you for creating a beautiful day. Thank you for allowing me to be part of your creation and most of all, for just being God. I welcome your presence and invite you to be in my morning, and my entire day. Lord, remind me of the accomplishments I have done, even the smallest ones that I do not think contain much significance. However, help me to remain humble and to not become "stuck up" about what I have done. Bless me and keep me always. I thank you for all you have done.In Jesus' name, amen.

Day Twenty-Seven

So be careful to do what the LORD your God has commanded you; do not turn aside to the right or to the left.
~Deuteronomy 5:32

There are countless distractions in the world to pull you away from success, your family, your career and its ultimate goal—your relationship with God. We need to stay focused.

I believe one of the biggest ways to avoid distractions, especially those targeted toward your relationship with God, is by not becoming curious about things that do not concern Him. How is that? Have you ever gone on the internet for a specific purpose? You turned on your computer or laptop to check your email, write a school report, or research something. Then, you saw a link or an email that was about a new Facebook message, a new sale, or a particular topic that peaked your interest? And from that you were redirected to a social networking site, some retail website, or something else of the sort, just to realize afterward, it distracted you from what you wanted to accomplish?

It isn't any different with God. When we concern ourselves with things which will not bring us closer to Him, we can become distracted by them. This is what the scripture above means by saying, "Do not turn aside to the right or to the left." Instead, concentrate. Have a goal, continue doing the work God instructed you to do and follow through with it.

Now, don't get me wrong. This doesn't mean you can't

enjoy doing something recreational. However, it does mean do not fall into activities that will bring you down and pull you away from the God you serve.

Today's Prayer:
Good Morning Lord,

Today, please help me to remain focused on your kingdom, your light and your love. Enable and equip me that I may not become distracted with the things of this world, but continue doing the work you have instructed me to do. God, for today and always, may I remain faithful in fulfilling the purpose you have planned for me. Thank you for all of this. In Jesus' name, amen.

Day Twenty-Eight

For I testify that they gave as much as they were able, and even beyond their ability. Entirely on their own, and they went beyond our expectations; having given themselves first of all to the Lord, they gave themselves by the will of God also to us. But since you excel in everything—in faith, in speech, in knowledge, in complete earnestness and in the love we have kindled in you—see that you also excel in this grace of giving.
~ 2 Corinthians 8:3,5,7

"Get a blessing, by giving a blessing." If you know me, or seen my Twitter and Facebook messages, or read anything I've ever written, this quote will be familiar.

It's something I've been saying for years.

We live in a selfish, greedy and uncompassionate society. I understand this doesn't speak for all, but collectively, it's true. People are always thinking and concerned about themselves —completely disregarding the welfare of others.

I love the first line (verse 3) which reads, "They gave as much as they were able...beyond their ability." How beautiful. It's rare to find a person who gives beyond your expectations; a person who goes the extra mile because they've given God their all and want to share what's left with you.

I'd like to challenge you today to be a blessing to others. God has blessed you abundantly. Why not use some of those blessings to bless others? My friend, Marie Wikle, the founder and owner of a nonprofit, Spreading Joy, has a wonderful slogan I love: "There's no joy, like spreading joy!" I love it because of its authenticity. The greatest joy is in giving; after all, God gave Christ for us.

Today's Prayer:
Good Morning God,

How are you? Thank you for giving so much to me and for giving us the best of gifts—Jesus Christ. God, help me today to have a heart that wants to give. Enable me to do so willingly and to want to bless others as you have blessed me. I invite you into my day and to be present within my life. Please help me to give the gifts of love and peace. In Jesus' name, amen.

Day Twenty-Nine

Whoever is patient has great understanding, but one who is quick-tempered displays folly.
~ Proverbs 14:29

Patience is more than a virtue—it is a characteristic everyone should have. Because it is required in almost every aspect of our lives, it is foolish not to make it part of our lifestyle. Relationships demand it, learning requires it and wisdom comes with it.

Every day people rush into situations because they lack patience. They settle for less because they refuse to wait for more options and in the end, realize the wisest decision was to have waited.

For example, how often do we jump to conclusions in a situation without being patient enough to let the other individual explain? We make bad conclusions based upon a small amount of information. In contrast, if we had only waited for the other person to speak, an argument could have been prevented through a mutual understanding. It is interesting that in chapter fifteen, Solomon writes: "A hot-tempered person stirs up dissention, but a *patient* individual calms a quarrel."

As you think about the times you were impatient in life, perhaps even today, ask yourself what benefits you received from it. Did the lack of patience hinder you or help you overall? If you were patient, could the situation have resulted in a better way? Practice patience; force yourself to wait and like anything else you do constantly, it'll become a habit.

Today's Prayer:
Good Morning God,

Please teach me how to be patient with others, with myself and for the things you have planned in the future for me. Allow me to take my time, not rushing into situations, and to understand that in being wise, I must learn to embody this characteristic. In Jesus' name, amen.

Day Thirty

No weapon forged against you will prevail, and you will refute every tongue that accuses you. This is the heritage of the servants of the LORD, and this is their vindication from me, declares the LORD.
~Isaiah 54:17

Many people question God when hardships arrive. Their faith wavers and they don't trust God as much as they did. After all, if God loved them and said He would always protect them, why are unfortunate events occurring? They lack the understanding that amidst their struggles God is still keeping and protecting their life.

Job, a servant of God, trusted the Lord in all things; he had unwavering faith and believed despite all predicaments, God would deliver him. It is because of his great faith that Satan had to first ask God for permission to harm him (Job 1:8-11). Before Satan even sent out the first attack against Job's life, God knew it was going to happen—he had granted permission. And with us, it's the same. So the next time you say "God doesn't understand," think differently.

As we progress through Job, chapter one, God gives consent for Job's faith to be tested under one condition: Satan cannot "lay a finger" on Job (Job 1:12). You see, God said Satan could turn Job's life upside down. Satan could take away things and destroy it; he could cause turmoil, pain, heartache, but he *could not* and *was not* allowed to touch Job's life. God may have permitted Satan to harm everything *in* Job's life, but He didn't allow Satan to harm Job. There's a difference.

In your walk with God, you will be tested and encounter struggles. Being a kingdom's child doesn't exempt you from problems. See the issues you are going through as an exam you know you are going to pass. Satan may test your faith, but as God's child, you've already received the victory!

Today's Prayer:
Good Morning God,

Thank you for protecting me. Thank you for not allowing any harm or danger, seen and unseen, to come against me. Please remind me that you are forever with me, protecting me always. I place my life into your hands. In Jesus' name, amen.

Day Thirty-One

Then the king asked, "What is it, Queen Esther? What is your request? Even up to half the kingdom, it will be given you."
~Esther 5:3

As we come to a close with *God in Your Morning*, I wanted to format today's devotion differently. I hope you don't mind. When Esther went before the king, she had a special request in her heart. She was nervous, scared, and perhaps even worried to ask the question she desired. And yet, we see the king welcomed her. He didn't address her as just Esther either, but "Queen Esther" saying whatever her heart so desired, he would give it her—even if it was half of his kingdom. I couldn't help but think with us and King Jesus it is the same way. Jesus told us we have not because we ask not (James 4:2). I could only imagine us being before the throne of God and King Jesus saying, "What is it, my beloved? What is your request? Even up to half the kingdom, it will be given to you."

Today, I don't know the request and the special desire you hold within you. I implore and encourage you to go before the throne of God and tell Him the very words you wish to say.

This past month, we have learned and talked about being with God. We are able to have a conversation with Him and have learned if we seek God, we will find Him. God listens to the prayers of the righteous. And in these 31 days, we've invited God into our morning each and every day.

In lieu of having a prayer for you to say today, I want you to create your own. Let it be from your heart, let it come out of your spirit. Speak to God.

Remember, He's listening.

Good Morning, God...

About Ashley Ormon:

Ashley Ormon is the editor-in-chief at *IN THE LIGHT* magazine. Her writing career began at age 16 when she was published in a poetry anthology. Since then, her work has appeared in international poetry collections, community magazines and the internet. When she isn't writing she spends her time speaking at events, reading, and doing photography. Her hope is for people to experience God through her words.

Connect with Ashley:

Twitter: @AshOrmon
Web: proverbsnwisdom.com/author/ashley

God in Your Morning:

If you've been blessed by this book, please recommend it to others. If you're on social media, you can even use the hashtag #GodInYourMorning. We would like to hear from you too! The publisher welcomes your comments and suggestions at contact@proverbsnwisdom.com. All messages to the author will be forwarded to her address.

Have Your Book Signed:

The author is always happy to sign books for readers. Send your book, along with a self-addressed stamped envelope and return postage to Proverbs & Wisdom, ATTN: Ashley Ormon, P.O. Box 3019, Garden City, NY 11531. Please make sure you include to whom the book should be made out.

About Proverbs & Wisdom:

Proverbs & Wisdom is dedicated to providing people with empowerment, encouragement, and enlightenment. It is the organization's mission to expose the love God has for all people, the saving grace all can receive through Jesus Christ, and to help bring lives closer to God.

For more information about Proverbs & Wisdom or to contact us, please visit us on www. proverbsnwisdom.com

Or write to us at:
Proverbs & Wisdom
P.O. Box 3019
Garden City, New York 11531
United States

Made in the USA
Charleston, SC
28 June 2014